DANIELLE FISHEL

girl gets real

A TEENAGER'S GUIDE TO LIFE

DANIELLE FISHEL

girl gets real

A TEENAGER'S GUIDE TO LIFE

BY DANIELLE FISHEL WITH MONICA RIZZO

Scholastic Inc.
New York Toronto London Auckland Sydney Mexico City New Delhi Hong Kong

Book design by Peter Koblish

ISBN 0-439-08788-0

12 11 10 9 8 7 6 5 4 3 2 1   9/9 0 1 2 3 4/0
                                                            23

Printed in the U.S.A.
First Printing December 1999

DEDICATION

First of all, I'd like to thank Scholastic for giving me the opportunity to write this book. Many thanks to Randi Reisfeld for
bringing this opportunity to me directly. I'm grateful for all the
years — past, present, and future — that I've been fortunate
enough to get to know her. I hope there will be more opportuni-
ties to work together.

To Monica Rizzo: I couldn't have been blessed with a better
co-author! You've become a friend of mine, and I look forward to
many more coffee/lunch dates in the future, when our meetings
will be for pleasure, not business!

I'd also like to acknowledge all the people who have helped
build my career over the years. My agent, Judy Savage, and all
the wonderfully talented people at The Savage Agency. You
guys are the best! My publicist, Scott Appel, who is a dear
friend and has managed to make PR events a blast! LOOK AT
THE SHEEEEEEP!! My mommy: the best darn manager anyone's every known! My daddy: the best darn money investor

anyone's ever known! How's that Hasbro stock? Pull my money out . . . let me spend it!!:-) Daddy and Mommy always know best . . .

On a more personal level I'd like to thank my wonderful mother, Jennifer (Becky or Miss Maguilicutti!); my incredible father, Rick; my beautiful brother, Chris; and my amazing Chihuahua, Tyson, for all the years of hard work, commitment, and dedication it has taken on all of their parts to help me fulfill my dream. None of these stories would have been the same without your guidance, friendship, love, and — most important — support. Next, I'd like to thank my bestest friends in the whole world, Jessica, Jamie, and Danielle. You are all inspirations to me and continue to keep me down to earth. You are true models of where beauty comes from: the inside out. I look forward to our lifelong friendships. Special thanks to my Ammas and Pappas, aunts, uncles, and cousins, who never let me forget how great and important family is. I love you with all my heart.

THE FANS!! To each and every one of you who bought this book and who follow and support my career, I can't thank you enough! REALLY, none of this would be possible without you! Last but certainly not least I'd like to thank the Lord for all the blessings He has given my family and me. I try every day to live my life in a way that would make You proud.

table of contents

INTRODUCTION   1

FAMILY   5

PETS   17

SCHOOL   27

SELF-IMAGE   37

TRUST, RESPECT, AND CROSSING THE LINE   47

HOBBIES, SPORTS, AND PASSIONS   61

FRIENDSHIPS   71

DATING   85

A HARD LESSON   97

ROLE MODELS   107

RELIGION & SPIRITUALITY   115

WHO I AM AND WHERE I'M GOING   125

ACKNOWLEDGMENTS

Many thanks to Randi Reisfeld for her guidance, Michael Eames for his love and support, and Scott Appel for his friendship. And a special thanks to Danielle for all of the laughs and ice-blended coffees.

— Monica Rizzo

INTRODUCTION

INTRODUCTION

I can't tell you how many times people have come up to me and told me how lucky I am to live such a glamorous life. They tell me how lucky I must be to wear great clothes, have any guy I want, and not have to worry about school. It's as if they think I'm Topanga Lawrence.

And you know what? That's not all true.

Yes, I'm an actress on a popular television show. And yes, I've met some pretty cool people. But honestly, my daily life is far from glamorous. I deal with the same issues in my world that everyone deals with. I have a curfew and an allowance. I've been grounded when I've been bad, and not every guy that I've liked has liked me back.

Plus, I'll let you in on a little secret. I've been known on occasion to battle a round or two with an unsightly, untimely pimple and I've been the victim of my share of fashion emergencies!

I decided to write this book for a couple of reasons. First of all, I do consider myself blessed, but not because I'm an actress. I feel blessed to be a part of such a loving, supportive family. And I have some very dear friends who make my world fun and interesting. It's these special people in my life who have helped shape and mold me into the person I am today. And thank goodness. I don't think I could do it on my own. So I wanted to share that with you.

Secondly, I wanted to show you that I'm just like any other teenage girl who's trying to learn what life's all about. And as you'll see, I've made my share of mistakes along the way. I've broken my parents' trust and I've done some things I'm less than proud of. But I've grown and I've learned from these experiences.

This isn't Danielle's little advice book. Rather, it's a glimpse into my life, my world, and how I deal on a day-to-day basis. I'm not perfect. But I'm always trying to be a better person. Growing up is hard. But maybe by reading about my world, you'll take away a greater understanding of your own.

FAMILY

FAMILY

My family is the most important thing in the world to me, and I'm not just saying that because it's a politically correct statement to make. I would never be the person I am today without their love and support and, for that alone, I am eternally grateful.

My mom has been my best friend since I was a little girl. Her name is Jennifer, and to say that she's the coolest is an understatement. Ever since I can remember, I've been able to talk to her about anything. I mean literally *anything*. We laugh together, cry together, get into arguments with each other like any normal mother and daughter. Most of all, we love to hang out together and buy new clothes, get manicures, eat lunch. We're planning a mother-daughter getaway to Minneapolis because there's some serious shopping there!

My dad, Rick, is a pretty neat guy, too. He brings out the tomboy in me. He taught me how to wrestle, how to throw a football, how to play tennis. We have some very special times together, like last year, when we went to the U.S. Open tennis tournament. My dad is an incredible player and has played in some pretty competitive amateur tournaments. Of course, the U.S. Open is for pros, so we were just spectators. On weekends, we'll go to the tennis courts in our neighborhood and play a game. He always kicks my butt! But someday . . .

My brother, Chris, is four years younger than I am and plays bass guitar and sings in a band. We also have a great relationship — though that's not always been the case. We used to fight about everything. And I mean everything. Once, we were in the car on a trip with our parents and we got into this huge fight in the backseat. Neither of us wanted the other looking out "our own" window. Chris started screaming and put his arms over his window and started yelling, "MOM! She's looking out my window!" My mom was not amused at all.

For a long time, having a younger brother meant, for me at least, having someone to torment. I used to try to get him in trouble, just to watch him scream and yell. Horrible, I know, but true, so true. One time we were both supposed to be in bed, and my brother had gone down the stairs and turned on the hall light. So my parents were sitting in the family room, and my mom got up and turned it off. Well, Chris ran back downstairs and turned it back on because he thought his room was too dark. My dad was a little annoyed, so he got up, turned off the light, and yelled, "Christopher, you stay in bed and get to sleep!" My mom can be pushed a little but when my dad reprimands us, we listen. So Christopher was scared and stayed in bed. But I couldn't resist, so I tiptoed down the stairs, turned on the light, and ran back up to my room as fast as I could. Oh, man, were my parents mad! They thought it was Christopher again and they started yelling at him. He tried to convince them he was innocent by claiming, "It wasn't meeeee!" I just stayed in my bed and giggled the whole time while he was getting yelled at. Wasn't I a mean big sister? I don't do that anymore, you'll be glad to know.

What makes my family so special to me, and especially my parents, is that they always listen to what I have to say. When I told my mom and dad that I wanted to be an actress, they didn't dismiss it as a crazy whim. They allowed me to pursue it. We sat down and talked over the process of how someone enters the acting world. It's so involved that I sometimes look back and can't believe my parents were so supportive.

You have to find an agent, which means going to lots of different talent agencies. The people at these agencies are really friendly but brutally honest. The reality is that thousands upon thousands of kids want to get into acting, which means lots of competition for one job. And if you know somebody who's connected to the business, you sometimes have an edge over someone who doesn't know anybody. We didn't know anybody, really.

I had a friend who had done some modeling, but that's it. So we schlepped up to Los Angeles to meet people and get pictures taken and see what possibilities existed for me. I was lucky that it didn't take long for me to get some work. After several months of driving back and forth to auditions, I was cast in a Barbie commercial for Mattel. In fact, I was the Mattel girl for a while, which was great because I got some really cool dolls!

After that, I started to get more work. My dad told me that when people are looking for work, no matter what the field, it's usually the first job that's the toughest to land. Then, once you are able to prove that you're capable of a job, you usually can get more work. Of course, as far as acting goes, that's not the way it always works. But like I said, I was lucky.

So I kept on working, doing commercials, and going to school. When I was eleven, I auditioned for a role on *Full House* — and I got it! I was so excited about that because I knew from going on so many auditions how difficult it was to get a part on a popular show, or on any show for that matter. It wasn't long after *Full House* that I was asked to audition for the part of Topanga on *Boy Meets World*. I was on cloud nine!

My family realized the incredible impact it would make on our lives, and they still allowed me to do it. But I was just a kid who landed a role on a really cool television show, so I never considered any fallout from pursuing acting. But now I realize how much they all sacrificed for me.

At the time when things first started happening, my family was living in Orange County, California, which is approximately sixty miles from Los Angeles. So when I started acting, my mom would have to drive me all the way up to LA, wait for me while I worked, and then drive me all the way back home. And she runs our house, making sure everything is taken care of — the clothes are clean, the meals are prepared, etc. — so this was an incredible burden. Some days we'd be gone all day, until nine or ten at night. My dad never got to see us, except on weekends. And my poor brother had to always come along with my mom and me because she couldn't leave him at home. All he wanted to do was play with his friends and be a normal six-year-old.

I think there was a time when things were hard for Chris because I was getting a lot of attention. My mom had to spend time with me because she'd have to be on set with me or chauffeur me someplace. And my dad was working. Chris would complain that he felt neglected and that he couldn't do what he wanted to do. And we all felt bad about it.

People always ask me if I feel like I missed out on my childhood by becoming an actress at a young age. And I really don't. I wouldn't change a thing. But when I think about Chris, I wish I could go back and make up for all the times he had to forego playing with his friends so that I could go to an audition. At the time, I don't think I realized how much he sacrificed for me.

It used to be a bone of contention between us. You know, we'd bicker back and forth, and he'd say I was my mom's favorite. And that's so not true. But I can see how he would have felt that way.

It's funny because people ask me all the time if Chris is jealous of me. I think at one time he might have been. But now? No way. We both have come into our own as individuals. Sure, I'm on a television show and he's not. But he can sing and play guitar and skateboard. I mean, he's awesome! I can't do any of that stuff! We're both really proud of each other and we don't have that sibling rivalry thing at all.

In fact, I'd say about four or five years ago our little brother-sister game-playing stuff subsided, and we became pretty good friends. I think it's just that we realized that family somehow is different than friends — you know, the bond is stronger. And since I've been driving for the past two years, we've become especially close because I can take him and his friends places. It's not a drag at all because I love driving. These days we can really talk to each other and trust each other, especially about stuff that we wouldn't necessarily want to talk to our parents about. I like to get his opinion on things and I know he likes to get mine because we always give each other honest answers.

I think it's because of my growing-up experience that I want to have a family of my own someday. My parents are such good parents, and I think I'll be a good parent, too. The thought of getting married and having kids really appeals to me. What doesn't appeal to me is having to deal with today's world. It seems like every other day you hear about a kid bringing a gun into school and shooting up everything in sight. People take drugs, steal from one another, hurt one another, kill one another. It's depressing, but it's our world, and it's something my

FAMILY

family and I talk about all the time. What will it be like when my brother and I are raising our families someday? Will our kids be able to go to public school like we did? I think good values begin in the home, and what I've learned from my family I will pass along to my kids, and so on. Not a day goes by, and I mean this from the bottom of my heart, that I'm not thankful for all that my family has done for me.

Random Thoughts

FIVE QUESTIONS PEOPLE ASK ME THE MOST:

1. What shampoo do you use?

I wash my hair with whatever shampoo is in the shower.

2. Who are you dating?

I'm dating a really nice guy.

3. What is it like to kiss Ben Savage?

Kissing Ben is part of my job. But I can think of worse jobs, if you know what I mean!

4. May I have your autograph?

Sure, I'll give you my autograph. Just ask.

5. Where did they come up with the name Topanga?

Topanga is the name of a place in Los Angeles. It's actually a canyon that has a hippie, earthy reputation. My character's parents were hippies, and so they named their child after it.

PETS

PETS

I guess it's obvious that I'm an animal lover, given that I posed with my dog, Tyson, on the back cover! I have had so many pets while I was growing up — hamsters, fish, lizards, and, of course, dogs. I think the thing I love most about having pets is their amazing loyalty. They don't care if you're fat, if you're ugly, if you have makeup on, or if you don't. They love you no matter what, and that unconditional love is what makes them so special because they're the only creatures who do that.

In many ways, my pets were my first friends. Joey was my first pet. He was a rat and he was the best. I remember the day we got him at the pet store and he was crawling all over me, very curious and affectionate. We'd put him in his cage and he'd do these little pull-ups on a bar inside. He'd eat food out of my hand and give me little kisses on my nose. I know it sounds absurd, but he was the sweetest, smartest rat in the world!

We used to leave his cage open so that he could run around the house, and he'd always go to his favorite hiding place under the couch. We totally knew he was there, but we'd play along every time. The minute we'd let him out of the cage, he'd scurry under the couch and wait for us to stand in the center of the room and call his name. "Jooooo-eeeeeey!" we'd yell. He'd come running out from under the couch toward us! I've never seen a rat that loved being with people more than Joey. And not only that, he had a really playful streak in him. You'd think that our dog, Tyson, wouldn't be afraid of a rat. I mean, even though Tyson is a small dog, he was, like, ten times Joey's size. But every time we'd let Joey out of his cage, Tyson would freak out and run away. It was the funniest thing because Joey caught on that Tyson was afraid of him, so he used to tease him all the time.

Joey's favorite thing was to go into the kitchen and take Tyson's dog food piece by piece. Tyson would be so mad, but he wouldn't do anything because he was afraid of Joey! So Joey would walk back and forth from the living room to the kitchen and take whatever he wanted, and Tyson would just pace around and huff and puff! Joey would just keep taking the food and storing it under the couch. There were massive amounts of food under there! We used to have such fun watching the two of them! When Joey died, we were really sad. Chris and I had a funeral for Joey, and we made him a tombstone. He was a special little guy.

You'll never guess what one of my other favorite pets was. A lizard! Who says girls don't like reptiles? Chris is a big lizard guy. One day, years ago, he started bringing home all these blue-bellied lizards that he found outside. Some of them were just a few inches long, and others were almost a foot long. I used to think they were gross until Chris showed me how gentle they really are. I started holding them all the time and, I have to say, they're pretty neat and very cute. Chris and I started going on these little excursions near our house to see how many lizards we could find. We'd catch them and look at them and pet them and then we'd let them go.

This became such a regular thing for us that Chris eventually got two collared lizards as pets from the pet store. They're called collared lizards not because they need to be on a leash, but because they have a marking on the skin around their neck that looks like a little collar. Or, from a woman's point of view, the marking looks like a choker necklace.

Our favorite lizard was named Bob, and he had such personality and energy. We'd put him on the floor, tap him on his tail, and watch him run around the kitchen on his little hind legs. He was awesome and *soooo* cute. I loved coming home from school and playing with him. But then one day he got really sick, and we didn't know exactly what it was, but we noticed that he just stopped eating. So my mom took Chris, Bob, and me to the vet. The doctor said, "Well, there's nothing we can do. Lizards just don't live that long."

Bob was going to die. But, the vet assured us, it was not because of anything we neglected to do. He was just old. We had him for a few years, and it was getting time for him to go. We wanted to make the rest of his life as comfortable as possible, so the vet said we could try to force-feed Bob by putting food in a syringe. So for several months, three times a day, my brother and I would mash up food and feed Bob with a syringe the vet gave us. Even at four o'clock in the morning, we'd wake him up, and he'd open his mouth, and we'd squirt food into it. He'd look at us with his sweet eyes, as if to say, "Thank you." We prolonged his life, and I think he knew without a doubt that we loved him.

Needless to say, I've always been a sucker for animals. They're such sweet creatures. My favorite pet ever? You guessed it — Tyson. He's a long-haired Chihuahua and he's *soooo* adorable. When I come home from a long day at work, Tyson runs to the front door to greet me and lick my face! It's such an amazing feeling to have a little friend like him. If I've had a bad day, like I bombed on a test or traffic was a nightmare and I'm totally stressed out, that little five-minute exchange with Tyson when I get home totally erases my bad mood. It's almost like he sees it as his job to make me happy. We play in the living room, cuddle on the couch, and watch TV together. We take naps, go for walks, kiss each other. He's definitely a member of the family, like the third-born child.

We also have Cassidy, a husky-Lab mix with one blue eye and one brown eye, whom I affectionately refer to as "the beast." She's huge, and we don't let her inside the house too often because she upsets Tyson. So she has the entire backyard to run around. She's a pretty dog, but I'm just not a big "big dog" person.

PETS

I like small dogs, and little Tyson fits on my lap. He's my honey. I've had him since he was only two pounds. He used to sleep in my arms, and I'd pretend he was my baby. I still do. I'd tell him secrets and sing to him. We've had him for ten years. Now that he's getting older, he's been having some heart problems, and that's really hard. The thought of not having him around forever makes me really sad. But I just think of all the happy times I've had with him, and I can't help but smile. I'll always have pets because they bring such an incredible amount of joy into my life.

Random Thoughts

WHAT IT MEANS
WHEN I CALL YOU MY FRIEND

When I call you my friend, that means you are somebody I can call at three o'clock in the morning and cry to. You're going to take time for me, and I'm going to take time for you. You're not going to blow me off or talk about me behind my back. You're going to keep my secrets. And I will do all of those things for you, too. That's what a friend is to me, and that's why I don't have very many. Friends are very special people, and I treasure the ones I have.

SCHOOL

SCHOOL

You know what the hardest thing about working full-time on a television show has been for me? It's been having to fit in school. Thank goodness I've graduated high school and can now budget my own time. Everybody at my school always thought I had it so easy because I'm an actress and I had a tutor on the set. But what they didn't realize is that I was working, learning lines, rehearsing all day, plus taking geometry quizzes and doing science experiments just like any other high school kid would do. So I got no break. The homework that my classmates had in my high school was the same homework I was given when I worked on the set with my tutor.

Let me explain. *Boy Meets World* tapes twenty-two episodes a year, and each episode takes one week to learn lines, rehearse, and shoot. So that means I was at work twenty-two weeks out of the year and thus was unable to attend classes at my LA high school. Our show tapes for three weeks straight, and then the whole cast and crew gets one week off. That week off is called hiatus. So the week that the show was on hiatus, I was back at my regular school, sitting in class, passing notes, hanging out in the cafeteria at lunch. Can you tell that my favorite part of school was the social aspect?

At first some people at my school — obviously not my friends — were a little resentful that I would breeze in and out on my off weeks. I could hear them whisper, "Oh, the princess is back." Even a couple of my teachers were a little annoyed with having to "deal" with me, and not because I was a difficult person, but because it meant that they had to do their lesson plans in advance and coordinate with my set tutor so that when I was working, I would be learning the same things as my friends. So it was a little strained and at times my feelings were hurt. I used to cry to my mom that I didn't want to go back to school.

It took a lot of convincing my parents to let me pursue acting. And when they finally saw that I was serious, they said to me, "Danielle, we'll let you do this. But if your attitude changes one bit, we'll pull you out of there so fast your head will spin." Now, any logical person knows that your head won't spin, it will merely turn side to side. Ha-ha! They meant business, and their underlying message to me was that I was not allowed to let my grades slip at all. Geez, no pressure.

So every day, whether I was at work or at school, the understanding with my parents was that I'd come straight home and do my homework. No phone, no television, no shopping, not a thing could be done until I finished my homework. And you know what? It wasn't a bad habit to get into. I know people who are, like, "I'm going to relax for two hours, go to the mall, get something quick to eat, watch my favorite show on TV, and then I'll do my homework before I go to bed." I don't know about you, but if I did all that stuff before I did my homework, I'd be exhausted, and the last thing I'd have is energy to concentrate on school. I hate having things hang over my head like that because then it becomes bigger than it really is, like a huge obstacle that you start to dread. It just feels better to have it out of the way.

Even after my parents stopped keeping tabs on whether or not I was doing my homework, I kept up my after-school ritual. I've always been the type of person who gets good grades — mostly B's. If I study, I'll get B's. But I have to work my butt off to get an A. I don't know why that is, exactly, but that's always been my pattern. And for the most part, that's fine with me. My parents have always had the understanding with my brother and me that as long as we tried our hardest, any grade we got was okay. Now, my parents are not bullies, but they know what I'm capable of based on the grades I've gotten over the years. So if I bring home less than a B, I know I'm going to get questioned.

Well, if there's one class that's always been a nightmare for me, it's science. If I never have to take another science class for the rest of my life, I'll be a happy girl. Well, when I was in junior high, I was having trouble with this one science class. No matter how much I'd study, I'd always get a C. It was completely frustrating because I was doing the best I could but not getting the ideal result. The teacher I had, who was really a nice man, used to make a deal with us when we had tests. If we ever got less than a C, he'd let us do a makeup test during lunchtime. It was kind of a second chance to improve your grade. So it meant sacrificing a little social time with friends, but it was worth it because it meant I could get a better grade.

Now here's the not so great part of the story. The first time I did a makeup test, I realized this was the way to go because he'd hand us back our original exams with the wrong answers marked. Then he'd give us the answer sheet so that we could see the correct answers before we retook the exam. We'd have, like, ten minutes to look things over and then, incredibly, he'd give us the test again! The exact same multiple-choice test!

So instead of reading the question and seeing the right answer and learning, I'd memorize a story starting with the letters of the right answers. Say the answers were A, C, B, D, A, B, D, E, A. I'd make up a little story that had those letters at the beginning of each word. So my story would go, "All Cats Bite Dogs And Bad Dogs Eat Ants." Really dumb, I know, but it worked. So I'd just memorize the letters and fill in the blanks on the test and get a hundred. And he'd be, like, "Danielle, you do so well the second time around."

I had this going on for a while. I mean, who wouldn't? It was so easy. I figured eventually he'd catch on, but he didn't. The first time I did it, I just laughed about it. But then, after the second time, I felt *soooo* guilty because he was so nice and unsuspecting. I began to see that devious wasn't the way to go because in the end, I was gaining nothing by it. Plus, if he ever found out, he'd be so disappointed in me. Not to mention my parents. And then I thought that even some of my other classmates would be upset because here they were, studying hard for each test, and I was slacking off, taking the makeup test, and getting as good or better grades than they were. So at the end of the year, I came clean and told my teacher. And he was, like, "Hmmm, I was a little suspicious because you'd do really well the second time around."

Thankfully, he was pretty cool about it and commended me for telling the truth, even if it was after the fact. The ironic thing about it is I didn't even get a better grade. I mean, I still got a C, so what was the point?! I'm happy to say that I've never cheated since. I guess I've become a little more ethical in my teenage years. And even better is the fact that I've graduated high school. So "Bye-bye, science class!"

Random Thoughts
WHAT BUMS ME OUT?

1. Getting into an argument with my parents. I don't like to fight. I like it when we all get along. It's not good for a person's soul to argue all the time.

2. Lying. I don't tolerate people who lie.

3. When you do something for someone, like send a card when he or she is having a bad day, and it goes unnoticed. I don't do things for people because I want them to notice me. But it's nice to get a smile or a hug acknowledging the gesture.

4. My friends are going off to college, and I feel kind of left behind. I know we'll stay in touch, but I'll miss them.

5. When I really want to be somewhere else, but I can't be because of another commitment.

SELF-IMAGE

This is me on the computer in the *Boy Meets World* schoolroom.

This is Ben and me on the student union set.
Ben is not only the co-star I'm closest to, but he's also one of my
real-life best friends. Isn't he cute?!

This is my wardrobe lady, Julie, and our huge mass of clothes for Topanga!
Wouldn't we all love to have a closet like that?!

Between takes of a scene our 2nd stage manager, DiDi Destefano, comes to help me with my lines! Thanks, DiDi!

This is my hairdresser, Laurie Heaps, putting some bobbie pins in my hair. Laurie is the best!

This is me getting my makeup done by my makeup artist, Annalisa. She's very creative and she's very good at keeping my foundation to a minimum I hate foundation!

SELF-IMAGE

Being a woman in today's world is not an easy thing. Now, I'm not about to mount some political horse and start waving a flag for feminism. But there are all kinds of reports and studies that have proven how men are paid more, on average, than women, or how women have to work harder than men at the same job.

And then there's the old body-image issue, one on which I have some very strong opinions. As much as I pride myself on being confident and intelligent, I have to admit, reluctantly, that I've fallen into the same trap that women have fallen into for years. I'm only eighteen, and already I can say that there is honestly not a single second of my day that I am not conscious of what my body looks like. I know a lot of girls look up to me as a role model. And I wish it weren't so, but I deal with the same things every other woman deals with. You know the drill: Is my butt too big in these pants? Does this dress flatter my figure? I'd better not eat too much or I'll gain weight and then nobody will like me.

When you think about it, it's so ridiculous, right? I mean, who cares? Yet millions of women get sucked into believing they should look like all those runway models in Milan. Well, first of all, not all of us are six feet tall and super skinny. And secondly, what would be so great about every woman looking the same? Our shapes are a small part of our whole as human beings.

I went through a really bad phase for a year or two and I'm not proud to admit it, but I had a very poor body-image thing going when I was younger. You'd think that being on a really successful show would make me happy — and I was, believe me — but I only felt more self-conscious as my body shot through puberty on national television.

Every time I'd look at myself, on or off camera, I'd start making mental adjustments. Five pounds here, a little more off the tummy, tone my arms. I'm not saying that wanting to improve your figure is a bad thing. But the way I set out to achieve that was wrong. I started eating improperly. For lunch I'd eat salads with no dressing and drink water or maybe have just a frozen yogurt cone — fat-free, of course. What made matters even worse was when I'd sit with my friends at lunch. Their typical meal consisted of two pieces of the greasiest cafeteria pizza, a bag of chips, a Snickers bar, and a soda. They'd scarf it down in no time and not give it a second thought. Me? I'd gnaw on a dry bagel and just look at them in awe. I couldn't believe they could eat like that and not gain an ounce!

SELF-IMAGE

I became very particular about what I would and wouldn't eat, even when I was on vacation. My mom has this rule that whenever you're on vacation you should do whatever you want, because it's your time to let go, live it up. And that goes for eating, too. Well, I've adopted that attitude now, but back then, a no-holds-barred eating mindset was out of the question. One year, my family went to Hawaii, and all I would eat was fruit. We went to a luau, you know, where they roast the pig and everybody feasts around an open fire. I just had some pineapple and a virgin piña colada. I somehow had convinced myself that if I ate full meals like the ones my friends ate at lunch I'd gain weight. So I kept on my salads-without-dressing-and-frozen-yogurt regimen.

It wasn't long before my parents got really worried. They sat me down on more than one occasion to tell me I wasn't eating right. I remember I just got really defensive about it. "Leave me alone!" I yelled at them. "I know what I'm doing and I'm fine!"

You see, I was the shortest of all of my friends. And the curviest. I perceived my rapidly developing hourglass figure as a sign that I was getting fat, which was understandable considering the fact that all of my friends at school were twigs. They were taller than me, thinner than me. They had no shape, no hips, no boobs — just tall and straight, up-and-down stick thin. Because I was so different, I think subconsciously I was trying to be like them.

It's funny because, at the time, when I'd look in the mirror, I'd see this person who was totally overweight and full of flaws. But I was the only one who saw that image. It was all in my head. Nobody on the show ever said they thought I was too fat. My friends never said a negative thing to me. In fact, my friends used to always compliment me and say how lucky they thought I was to have a figure.

I don't know precisely when I snapped out of this little phase. I think it was perhaps around the time that I began to work out with a personal trainer and, as a result, I started learning more about how proper nutrition could give me the energy I needed for my workouts. When I finally started eating well, I put on a couple of pounds and I didn't worry because I knew that if I kept working out, I'd be healthier in the long run. One thing that really helped me was when I was talking to some of my guy friends about it. I was semi-whining that I'd put on a few pounds and wasn't as skinny as I had been just a month earlier. And they were honest with me and said, "Danielle, we don't mean to upset you, but you looked horrible. You were too skinny. You have a much better body now and you look healthy now." I can't tell you how much that boosted my confidence.

I've learned so much more about nutrition and exercise and how the two can work in tandem with a person's body type. I enjoy myself when I eat. I just do it in moderation. I love turkey burgers and french fries, just not every day. And if I go to a birthday party and there's cake, I'll eat one piece, not three.

SELF-IMAGE

There's nothing wrong with that. And I love working out because it makes me feel stronger and more confident.

When I go out of the house, I usually feel better if I've washed my face, brushed my teeth and my hair, and maybe put on a little makeup. I don't spend hours on end getting ready to leave the house. But I find that if I just do a little bit to make myself presentable in public, even if I'm wearing sweats, I feel better. And it makes sense, really. It's funny the little things you can do to boost your self-image and improve your everyday attitude.

Sure, I still wish I was a little thinner or a little taller. There's an extra five pounds I'd love to get rid of, but I'm not going to kill myself over it. It's only five pounds! I like the person I've become and I'm not going to sacrifice that just because my jeans might look a little better on me. Get real! There're days when I feel like that and then there are days when I think, "You've got it, flaunt it!" I've now learned to embrace the fact that I'm different. I have my own shape, my own striking features just like everyone else, and I'm comfortable with myself and my body.

Random Thoughts
HOW DO I DEAL WITH REJECTION?

I try to totally let it roll off my back and not affect me because most often when a person deals with rejection, it isn't personal. Let's say, for example, I am going on an audition, which is the entertainment industry's form of a job interview. Sure, if I don't get the part, I'll be a little bummed. In fact, it's happened to me lots of times. But I know that it wasn't because they didn't like me. It's rarely that. It's timing, it's climate, it's something that's out of my control. The same goes for dating. If I like a guy and he doesn't like me back, I'm not going to bawl my eyes out in my bedroom. Just because someone doesn't feel the same way about me, doesn't mean I'm not a good person with a lot to offer. So I don't sweat it.

TRUST, RESPECT, AND CROSSING THE LINE

TRUST, RESPECT, AND CROSSING THE LINE

I just described to you how wonderful my parents are, but in all honesty, I haven't always agreed with them. And after all, what kid does totally agree with everything his or her parents say?

Now let me give you a little background. My mom and dad are pretty cool, and we've always had the understanding that if there's anything I need to talk about with them, I can. Basically, they've always said that no topic is off limits. That's easier said than done. I mean, when I was eleven or twelve, I could tell my parents all about my day over dinner. I'd be, like, "Oh, in second period, so-and-so did this, and so-and-so got into trouble in history class for passing notes, and blah, blah, blah." I used to blabber on and not give it a second thought.

Then I got a little older, I was in ninth, then tenth grade, and I realized my parents didn't need to know everything about my day. A little selectivity isn't such a bad thing, you know.

I'd probably say I'm a wee bit closer to my mom because we've got the female bonding thing going on. So I can push her a little more than I can my dad when, say, our opinions don't jibe. With my dad, when the answer is no, it's no. But it's a little bit different with my mom. I pretty much know where the boundary lines are drawn, but sometimes I feel the need to test things out, if you get my drift.

Let me give you an example. A couple of years ago I was dating this really cool guy. I was fourteen and a freshman, and he was eighteen and a senior, so there was a four-year age difference. My parents weren't too comfortable with that, but they met him and felt he was a good guy, so they let me date him. Well, one day, he and I wanted to go to Disneyland. And in order to go, we would have to miss the last half of the school day — it was a Friday night — and drive down. My mom said I could go, but that I had to be home by midnight. Now, usually my curfew is either at eleven or midnight, depending on the circumstances, like if it's a weeknight or a weekend, where I'm going, what I'm doing, etc. So this time, I thought maybe the circumstances would warrant a little bit of latitude on my mom's part.

Hmmmm, I thought. *Time to bargain, Danielle.* So I said to my mom, "How about we leave the park at midnight?" And my mom said, "Home by midnight or you're not going at all. And that's final."

When I look back on it, my mom was being pretty darn reasonable considering I was only fourteen and I was going all the way to Disneyland from LA, which is an hour and a half away. But at the time I didn't see the logic behind what she was saying, so I just agreed, "Yeah, okay, midnight." And then I ignored her. Big mistake.

We went to Disneyland, and the day totally flew by. We had an amazing time and at midnight we got in the car and started driving back home. I have a pager that I always keep with me and about ten minutes after midnight it went off. It was my mom. I ignored her page. Fifteen minutes later it went off again, this time with a 911 after the number, which means it's urgent. I still ignored it.

So we got to my house, and it was about 1:30 in the morning, and there was my mom in her robe at the front door. She screamed at me, "Where the hell have you been? I've been worried sick about you!" She completely flipped out, and rightly so. But in the process, she woke up my dad. Not good. Now both of them were angry at me, telling me how irresponsible I'd been (they were right), telling me how disrespectful I'd been (right again), and how I was going to get grounded for a long time (gulp). I was never so scared in my life.

The next day my punishment was laid out for me — I was grounded for a month. In my house being grounded means no TV, no phone, no stereo, no shopping, no after-school events — nothing. I went to school, came home, did homework, went to bed. And to tell you how strict my mom could be, at the beginning of that summer our family had planned a trip to Hawaii. I had only four days left of being grounded and I thought I'd get off — you know, credit for time already served. But no. Instead, my mom said, "Being in Hawaii doesn't count. You're going on vacation with us and you can have a good time, but just know that when we get back home, you still have four days left, young lady." Yikes, can you believe that?! I was on my best behavior in Hawaii and, when we got home, my mom decided that I didn't have to make up those four days. But during the whole trip I thought otherwise.

So you think I would have learned my lesson, huh? Wrong. No sooner had that blown over than I broke a rule again. My parents are very strict about my brother and me not smoking or drinking. And frankly, those things don't appeal to us. But you know how everybody is doing something and you know it's wrong or you don't necessarily want to do it but because everybody is doing it you think it won't hurt? Well, I fell into that trap. I didn't exactly give in to peer pressure, but I did follow the crowd when I tried smoking.

Honestly, I wasn't really into it. But a lot of people that I work with smoke. One day, I was hanging out with them and I just picked up a cigarette and started smoking. I don't know why. I guess I just wanted to see what it was like, plus a little part of me thought it was kind of cool. I kind of liked the thrill of doing something your parents say you can't do, combined with the fact that I was hanging out with some older people and fitting in. I did this for a little while and, sure enough, I started to smell like smoke.

TRUST, RESPECT, AND CROSSING THE LINE

Needless to say, my mom caught on quickly, and she called my on-set teacher and asked if he'd ever seen me smoke. He had. I was busted. When I got home, my mom was waiting for me with strict instructions. "I'm sorry to do this to you, but dump out your purse right now," she told me. So I did and, luckily, there was nothing in there. But she wasn't fooled for a minute. "So how long have you been smoking?" she asked me. I couldn't lie, but I tried. "I don't smoke," I said in a nonconvincing I've-been-busted voice. But she could smell it on me. In fact, nobody smokes in my family, and the smell of smoke drives my mom nuts, so she knew instantly that I was lying.

When my dad got home, he flipped out. I was grounded for two weeks. In fact, this all happened on a Friday, and the next day there was a big dance at school, and I was so bummed that they weren't going to let me go. I had plans with my boyfriend at the time, and my dad wouldn't even let me call him. My dad actually called him and said, "Danielle has been smoking, and she's not going to be able to go to the dance with you tomorrow night." I was totally humiliated. And even worse than that, I was ashamed that I had ruined my boyfriend's weekend plans.

Well, after being grounded for two weeks, you'd think I would have learned my lesson. And I did. Kind of. For four months, I didn't have a single cigarette. It wasn't like I was addicted or anything. But I was following the rules until I went to visit a friend who lives far away, so we don't see each other all the time. We were hanging out. She had gotten into this huge argument with her mom earlier that day and when I got there, she said, "Let's get going, I need a cigarette."

I started laughing at her because one, this girl is a Mormon and two, she doesn't smoke! I was, like, "C'mon, you tried one cigarette in your life. You must be kidding."

Nope, she wasn't kidding. She pulled up to a gas station to buy a pack of cigarettes. Then she insisted that we go behind the building and smoke because, she said, "My parents know everybody in this town and if anybody sees me I'm dead." In the back of my mind I was thinking, *Hmmm, maybe this isn't such a good idea.* It's that weird, in-the-pit-of-your-stomach feeling that tells you when something is right and something is wrong. I ignored it, and together this girl and I went around the corner and lit up our cigarettes. No big deal, we took a few puffs and sat on the trunk of her car, trying to act cool. Then this cop car pulled up, and my friend flipped out. That little feeling in the pit of my stomach returned. But then, I thought, *My God, we're only smoking cigarettes.*

Little did I know that there's an ordinance of some sort forbidding minors from smoking cigarettes. It's actually illegal for minors to be in possession of tobacco, so the cop started writing us citations. All of a sudden we didn't feel so cool anymore. We were both freaking out, begging the cop not to give us the tickets. All I could think about was my parents and how mad they were going to be. They trusted me not to smoke again and here

TRUST, RESPECT, AND CROSSING THE LINE

I was, caught in action by the police, no less. And my friend was freaking out even more because her father is the bishop of the Mormon church. But no matter how much we tried to play upon his sympathy, the cop kept writing. He handed us our tickets, and it might as well have been a death sentence. I couldn't even imagine how long I was going to be grounded when my parents found out.

Now, these citations are not like parking tickets that you can just pay for out of your allowance without anybody knowing. I wish it would have been that easy, you know, write a check to the county, send it in, end of story. Not this time. Because we were minors, in addition to a fine, these tickets came with an assigned court date in which we would have to appear before a judge with our parents. Not only would I have to go with my parents, but it was in Orange County, which, as you know from my Disneyland adventure, is a ninety-minute drive from my house in LA.

So we got back into my friend's car, holding our tickets and panicking about how we were going to deal with this little dilemma. We decided to lie. So we concocted this whole story about why we got these tickets. We decided we would tell our parents, "Look, we weren't smoking, but some kids we were talking with were, and so the cop cited everybody." We were convinced it would work. We drove back to my friend's house, told her folks, and after a brief question-and-answer session, they believed us. Next up were my parents, who wouldn't be so easy to fool based on my history.

My mom came to pick me up the next day, and I started telling her the story my friend and I had told her parents. And my mom being the type of person who has to know everything started asking questions because she was skeptical. Like a detective, she started finding little flaws in my story. Every time I tried to dig myself out of a jam, I'd incriminate myself further. My mom wasn't totally convinced that a police officer could actually cite my friend and me if we weren't the ones smoking. So after we got home, my mom called my friend's mom and the two of them concluded that something wasn't quite right. So they each called us back in for questioning and that's where things fell apart. My friend caved in under the pressure and confessed everything to her mom. But before she could tell me she had done that, my mom got to me. I perpetuated the lie. I kept up with our original story. Busted. My mom knew everything, and I was grounded for a month.

Getting grounded wasn't such a big deal. I could live without TV, the phone, my stereo. What was truly horrible about this was that I had broken my parents' trust. I had disappointed them and, for the first time ever, I didn't know how I could fix it. Not only had I given them my word that I would never smoke again, but I had tried to deceive them only to save myself. In the end, it actually made things much worse. My mom even said to me on the last day I was grounded, "Don't think just because your punishment is over that you have my trust back." God, that cut like a knife. I still feel horrible when I think about it. It took many months before my mom felt she could let me go out and not have to worry about what I was doing. Having my parents' trust means a lot to me, and I've worked hard over the past year to show them that I am responsible and trust-worthy.

We have a "no questions asked" policy in our house, which basically means if I'm somewhere where people are drinking or participating in irresponsible behavior, I can call my parents any time of the day or night and they will pick me up and take me home. Thankfully, I've never had to take them up on that offer, and the reasons are pretty simple. Number one, I don't hang around irresponsible people. I choose my friends wisely and our value systems are the same. Secondly, if I ever have a doubt that something I'm doing might be wrong, I listen to my soul, my gut. The first thing that enters my mind isn't, *I might get grounded for this.* It's, *Wow, my parents would not be happy with this.* That always helps me make up my mind if I'm ever faced with a decision. If *no* is the answer to *Would this make my parents happy?* then what I'm doing is wrong, and I don't do it.

I think a lot of people, yours truly included, fall into the trap of going along with the crowd from time to time. But it's really important to do what's right for you. My mom has this goofy ex-pression, *Just because everybody else is jumping off the bridge doesn't mean that you have to, too.* I don't know about you, but I don't know too many bridge-jumpers. What she's really been trying to say is just because everyone else is doing something, like smoking, doesn't mean that I should, too. So now I don't. In fact, I can't believe that I did it because it's really a gross, smelly, unhealthy habit. As I've grown up, I've been faced many times with the question *Do I want to be a leader or a follower?* I much prefer being a leader, thank you.

Random Thoughts

THESE THINGS MAKE ME HAPPY:

1. A night at home with my family.

2. My dog, Tyson.

3. Frozen yogurt.

4. Looking at photo albums and yearbooks.

5. Sleeping in.

6. Jamie, Jessica, and Danielle.

HOBBIES, SPORTS, AND PASSIONS

HOBBIES, SPORTS, AND PASSIONS

People who know me know that I am a really physical person. The other night I arm-wrestled my dad, and he kicked my butt! Of course! I always hope that someday I can beat him. I guess I was born with that competitive nature. My favorite sports are tennis and football. I can watch them for hours at a time, live or on television. And I play them both very well.

I started playing football with the *Home Improvement* boys when I was twelve. *Boy Meets World* and *Home Improvement* both shot on this big production lot at the Disney studios in Burbank, California. Our studios were right next door to each other and, when we'd go on breaks, we'd hang out in this recess area where there was a basketball hoop and enough room to play touch football or soccer.

I was the only girl playing with Jonathan Taylor Thomas, Zachery Ty Bryan, and Taran Noah Smith. So needless to say, I got toughened up hanging with that bunch. I also became really good and, still to this day, I can throw a football on target better than some boys. I fantasize every now and again that I'll become a quarterback of a women's football team someday.

I've always found sports to be the key to my success, so to speak. Most of my friends aren't as into sports as I am. They are cheerleaders, so they're very athletic. And my friend Jamie will watch football with me. But for the most part, I've been a tomboy on my own.

I'm very blessed to have a split personality when it comes to that. One moment I can be out in the mud, no makeup, hair in a ponytail, roughing it up with the guys during an intense game of football. The next moment I can go inside, shower, change into a pink dress, put on makeup, style my hair, and be a total lady. I fit into both crowds very nicely, which worked well with my guy friends. They loved that I was so into sports that I was just as competitive as they were. Yet if I went out on a date, the boy knew he was taking out a girl and not a total jock.

I treasure the time I have to get physical, athletically speaking, because it's such a release of energy. I never really got into arts-and-crafts hobbies. Most of my hobbies involve some sort of athletics like kickboxing or weightlifting, because it makes me feel so good. Number one, I like doing it. And number two, it's a great way to build my body and my mind. I also like to write in my journal and send E-mail to my friends. When I express myself in writing, I find that that's a great way for me to clear my mind.

And then there's my other favorite hobby — shopping. It's neck-and-neck with sports. If I have free time, you can bank on it that I'm either working out or in a mall! If there's a mall within five miles of wherever I am, I'll find it. Give me an hour, and I'll spend and spend and spend.

Because of my love for shopping, though, my mom gives me a weekly allowance. (See, I told you my parents treat me like a normal teenager.) I used to get my allowance and spend it all right away. Then I'd be stuck for days without cash. So I got smart and started to budget my money. My mom helped me open my own bank account. And every week after she'd give me my allowance I'd deposit some of the money in my account. I learned the concept of planning and saving for what I really wanted, whether it was a new pair of platform shoes or a new purse.

I'm very much into buying new clothes. But I also like to spend my money on little treats here and there, like taking a friend to dinner or buying some new CDs. Music is probably by far my biggest passion. I have more CDs than anyone I know. And I can sing the songs off any one of them. Every chance I get I'm at the record store checking out what's new. I love rap and hip-hop, pop, and some alternative rock. I went through a big Beatles phase for a while, and then some oldies.

But rap and hip-hop is where it's at for me. There's no music I enjoy more.

I love being able to buy little things for my family, too. As much as I love shopping for myself, I've found that you can only have so much clothing and jewelry. It can get old fast when you're constantly buying things for yourself. I love the surprised look on my mom's face when I bring her a little gift, like a new pair of earrings or a bouquet of flowers.

Recently I've begun volunteering to help raise money for charities. A lot of the time I show up and sign autographs and pose for pictures. It's not hard and it's such a great way to meet some really nice people. I find "celebrity" to be kind of strange in a way. After all, I'm just a teenager with an allowance, a curfew, and a little brother. Oh, yeah, and I'm on a TV show. It's because my job is so different from what most other teenagers are doing that it gets so much attention. So I've decided that I'm going to use my celebrity to help people. If that means signing autographs for an hour, I'll do it.

One time a young boy named Matt from the Make-A-Wish Foundation came to our show. The Make-A-Wish Foundation is a charity organization that helps make chronically ill kids' dreams come true. This boy's wish was to spend the day with the *Boy Meets World* cast. It was so neat to meet him and show him where I work. Matt kept saying how much we all made his day. Little did he know how much he made *my* day! It was so rewarding to be able to help someone fulfill his or her dreams. I'm finding more and more that I like and want to help others any way I can. So I guess you could say charity work has become a new hobby of mine. I'm hoping I can ignite some interest with my friends, too. What we do today will make a difference in our future, our children's future, and so on. Volunteering and giving to others will fulfill you in a way that no shopping mall excursion could ever satisfy.

Random Thoughts

MY PET PEEVES

I'm really an easy person to get along with. But I do have my limits. For instance, I can't stand clutter. If something is messy, I can only tolerate it for about a day before I start cleaning like a maniac. And the bathroom *must* be clean at all times. No ifs, ands, or buts about it!

I also hate when somebody says he or she is going to do something and then never does it. I'm a pretty focused person, so if I give my word, I'm not going to go back on it.

I've described my home life in this book — now take a pictorial peek.
This is me and Tyson in the backyard.

This is my real-life closet. A little smaller than Topanga's, right? I have most of my clothes organized by color.

The treadmill! It's probably my least favorite form of exercise, but it sure is good for toning! I usually don't look this happy while working out... the camera just caught me at a good moment!

This is my vanity mirror, where I put on my makeup.
See how my hair is up in that banana clip?
If you see me on the street, that's what my hairstyle will be! I hate my hair down!

My honey! This is my precious puppy, Tyson!
He doesn't really like the water, but I do! I'll protect you, Ty-Ty!

We live in a quiet suburb of Los Angeles; this is our backyard pool.

This is one of my favorite spots in my house: the fireplace.
I love to make some tea and sit down here with a good book.
Maybe not during the summer, but during the winter it's great!

FRIENDSHIPS

FRIENDSHIPS

I consider myself pretty lucky because I've had the same group of friends since I was in the sixth grade. I started acting when I was young, but for the most part, my close friends knew me before I was on *Boy Meets World*. It wasn't like people were asking for my autograph or anything, but it was just different after I got on the show. I'm glad that the people who knew me before have stuck by me. And I've stuck by them.

Basically, I have three really close girlfriends — Jessica, Danielle, and Jamie. These are the three people, outside of my family, who I can totally be myself with. I can confide in them, laugh with them, cry with them. And they can do the same with me.

Jessica and I have known each other since kindergarten. When I was ten, my family moved from our house in Orange County, California, to Los Angeles, and it was really hard for Jessica and me. She lived just a couple of houses down the street from me, and we saw each other constantly. When my parents said we were going to move, I got really scared that Jessica and I would lose touch. But we didn't. My mom and dad knew how important it was for my brother and me to keep our friends, so they promised that after we moved we'd still be able to take trips on the weekends to visit with them. Our neighborhoods were a ninety-minute drive apart, so it wasn't like we saw each other all the time.

Still, over the years, Jessica and I have managed to stay in really close touch. We talk on the phone, write letters, send E-mail. Now, because we've both been so busy with school and work, we only see each other every other month, for two or three days at a time. Because we've known each other for so long and we've maintained our friendship over the years, we can usually pick up right where we left off. We don't have to talk every day in order to be friends, and it's really neat. I know we'll always be in each other's lives because we are so connected. Our friendship has grown in so many ways and withstood distance that no matter where we go, we'll remain friends.

The same goes for Danielle and Jamie. I used to think that quantity was better than quality when it came to friends. Man, was I wrong. At one point, I had fifteen so-called "best friends." I thought the more people I knew the better off I would be. It was really important for me to be a social butterfly and know what everybody was doing every minute of the day. It became even harder once I started *BMW*.

FRIENDSHIPS

As I mentioned earlier, I would go to school on my "off" weeks from the show. When I got to junior high school, my core group of friends treated me the same, but other people at school treated me badly. I overheard this one kid say in the hall one day, "Oh, the princess came back to grace our classroom for a week. Isn't she special?" I could sort of see why he would feel that way because he didn't know that I still had to do my school-work while I was working on the set. But I never defended my-self to him or to any others who whispered mean-spirited comments behind my back. I just took it.

When I'd get home, I'd explode to my mom and beg her to please let me just be tutored like some other kid actors I knew. They went to our set classroom every day and didn't have to deal with the disruption that I dealt with. But she insisted that my life be as "normal" as possible. What's so normal about being teased every day?

I kept going to my regular junior high, even though I really didn't like it. One thing is for certain, though. I learned how to interact with all sorts of people. I have to applaud my mom for making me stick with it. It would have been so easy to let me continue being schooled on set. But instead, I learned how to deal with many social situations. Whenever I would hear some-one whispering about me, or anyone for that matter, I'd think of what my mom told me. She said that when you hear someone gossiping or making catty remarks, you have to consider the source. I mean, chances are good that anyone who is like that is someone you don't want to be friends with anyway. So why even pay attention to what he or she says? It's not even worth stooping to that level and trying to compete. Just walk away. That's what I did and it worked.

When I hit high school, I felt like I was a new woman. I don't know why, but somehow, going to a new school gave my friends and me a new perspective on life. We made new friends and started dating a bit. It was really cool. Of course, we had to deal with some growing pains.

I found that in high school, there were some people that I didn't want to hang out with. They were the people who were gossiping about others behind their backs. You know, we'd all be sitting around the lunch table in the cafeteria and someone would get up to get a drink or go to the bathroom. And the catty remarks would begin. "Can you believe she's wearing that?" Or "Oh, man, did you see her flirting with so-and-so in gym class today?" I became self-conscious and afraid to leave the table for fear that they would start talking about me.

This kind of situation made me uncomfortable then and still makes me uncomfortable today. I started hanging out with some of the older kids in school, juniors and seniors, because I found that they were a little less critical of people. This ruffled some feathers with my friends, but I didn't care. And I'm sure I was talked about when I started to drift into a direction that was more comfortable. And you know what? So be it. I don't get caught up in what other people say about me. Life's too short to worry about petty things like someone being mad at me because I didn't sit at her lunch table, or I didn't wear an outfit that she approved of. If I like something, I'm going to wear it.

I don't understand why people feel the need to be so judgmental. I'm one of the least judgmental people. If I make friends with someone, it's not because she wears cool clothes or hangs out with the most popular crowd in school. It's because of the way I'm treated and because I'm accepted, faults and all. I've become close with all of the people I work with because they accept me for who I am. I can go in some days in sweats and no makeup and never hear a word about it. My philosophy is if it makes you happy and you're not hurting anyone, do what you want.

Sorry, I got on a little tangent there. But the moral of my story is that I soon learned that the word *friend* meant something more to me. Remember when I said quality is more important than quantity? Well, it's true. Growing up I've come to learn that my free time is important to me. I used to make myself crazy trying to call everyone I knew every night, do my homework, make the rounds in the halls in between classes to see who's doing what. I was exhausted at the end of the day! I wasn't happy but I didn't realize it. So I started to step back a bit. And not all of my friends understood. Just like when I branched out in the lunchroom to make new friends, they thought something was wrong with me.

But I was fine. I just realized that I had to start making myself and my *real* friends a priority. And how did I know who my real friends were? They were the people who listened to what I said and understood. I remember Jamie and I had this long-standing plan to get together on a Sunday and spend all day at the mall, shopping and getting a vanilla ice blended.

But when Friday afternoon rolled around, I just had no energy. I had been working all week and I was more than a little behind in my schoolwork. I was honest with her and asked if we could reschedule, and she was so great. She said, "Yes, of course, we can reschedule. Is everything okay? You sound so stressed." I was so touched that she actually asked me how I was. Even though she was disappointed, she didn't fly off the handle and tell me what an awful friend I was for canceling at the last minute. I was more important to her than the activity. That's a true friend.

I've been there for Jamie, too, because that's what friends do for one another. And you don't keep score, you just do it automatically. I kind of follow a code when it comes to friends: (1) I always try to be honest; (2) I don't gossip; (3) I'm there for a friend at three in the afternoon or three in the morning; and (4) I never let a guy get in between us.

I had to learn number four the hard way.

One time I got into a huge fight with my friend Jennifer because she started dating my friend Michael. She developed this cocky attitude and wouldn't talk to me. I felt that she thought she was better than me and that she was trying to steal all of Michael's time. So I did something so immature I'm embarrassed to admit it. I cut out a magazine article and stuck it in her locker. It was one of those quizzes. I think the headline was something like HOW TO TELL IF YOUR FRIEND IS A LOSER. Isn't that harsh? I even made it worse because I circled all of the bad "loser" answers on the quiz. It was really mean, and it made her cry. It's probably the one "friend" thing I've ever done that I'm ashamed of. If someone had ever done that to me, I would have been so hurt. I apologized to Jennifer like you would not believe, and we eventually made up. We even laughed about how petty I was. I still see her around from time to time, and we get along great. Even now, I feel the need to apologize. But she just laughs it off.

When you hurt someone's feelings like that, it's difficult to ask for forgiveness. I was lucky that Jennifer saw through the absurdity of my actions. It was so out of character for me to do that. But sometimes friends hurt each other's feelings without realizing it. That's why it's important to communicate properly. If something bothers me about one of my friends, I'm going to tell her, no matter how hard it is. And it's hard because basically you're opening yourself up to someone and confronting her about something that she said or did that upset you.

My friend Jamie is pretty good with communication. The minute something comes up that she needs to discuss, she tells me. There was this one time we were talking on the phone, and

I was venting about work. I was talking and she was listening, but I thought she was passively listening. You know, she would go "Uh-huh. Hmmm. Are you serious?" So I said, "I guess you wouldn't understand because you're not in the same business." And I ended the conversation. Now, I didn't mean to be hurtful. In fact, I thought I was being perceptive. I assumed that what I was talking about wasn't interesting to her or was something she couldn't relate to.

I was wrong — and she told me about it.

Later that night, Jamie wrote me an E-mail telling me that my little "you wouldn't understand" comment upset her. She said that when I dismissed the conversation with that little comment, it was as if I was shutting her out of my life, implying that her life wasn't as glamorous as mine. I certainly didn't intend for that comment to carry those implications. Thank goodness she told me how she felt. I told her that sometimes when she talks about going off to college, *I* feel shut out. It's something I can't relate to because when she's gone, I'll still be in LA working on the show.

We actually talked for a long time and discovered that there were things about each other that we really didn't know much about and if we hadn't said anything and discussed it, we would have kept on hurting each other. After that, I felt better than ever about our friendship. I think it only made us closer. I'll miss her when she's away at college in Michigan. But we'll stay in touch. After all, that's what winter, spring, and summer breaks are for. And if I want to, I can go visit when I'm off work.

And speaking of work, I've made some great friends there, too. Will Friedle (Eric), Rider Strong (Shawn), Matthew Lawrence (Jack), and the gang are so cool. We've had so much fun growing up together. And Ben Savage (Cory) is very special to me. We've become so close because of playing girlfriend and boyfriend on the show. We hang out quite a bit, and I know we'll be friends for a long time.

I've always had a lot of guy friends — I work with four of the hottest guys on TV! But seriously, I never thought it was a problem for girls and boys to be just friends. And it really isn't a problem, as long as both parties are on the same page. When you get older, it's sometimes difficult to maintain boy/girl friendships because often one person has stronger feelings or intentions than the other. I was naive about it for a long time. I had this one guy friend who treated me like a queen. I was twelve or thirteen at the time, and we'd hang out at school and do homework and go to school dances — all just as friends. Or at least that's what I thought.

Then one day we were hanging out at my house and my phone rang. It was another of my guy friends, and we talked for a minute or two because, of course, I already had a friend over. I wanted to be polite, you know. Well, right before I hung up, we playfully said "I love you" to each other. I didn't think it was a big deal, frankly. But my friend who was over got so mad at me.

"How can you say I love you to someone like it doesn't mean anything?" And I said, "It does mean something. I love all my friends, including you."

At the time, I thought he was totally out of line for questioning me. But now I look back and I see that maybe I did cross a line. Obviously the guy who was over at my house had feelings for me and was a little crushed to learn that we weren't on the same page. Of course he was a little jealous.

Needless to say, there are definite boundaries that you shouldn't cross when you're friends with a boy. You don't hold hands, you don't spend every waking minute together, and you certainly shouldn't be saying "I love you" to him! In essence, I was sending both guys mixed signals. Now that I'm in a relationship, I'm even more sensitive to what I say and do when I'm in mixed company. I don't want anyone to get the wrong idea. Most important, I wouldn't want to upset my boyfriend. If I heard him flirting or acting playful on the phone with another girl, I might get a little peeved. That's my barometer. If the tables were reversed . . . how would I feel? That's a good way to look at life in general. I figure if I stick to that basic philosophy, I'll avoid a lot of unpleasant situations.

Random Thoughts
IF SOMEONE WAS GOSSIPING ABOUT ME

If I found out someone was gossiping about me, I would probably ignore it until the rumors started becoming detrimental to my everyday existence. I don't care what people think about me, so it would have to be pretty bad for me to take any type of confrontational action. Nine times out of ten, it'll never get that bad. But if it did, I would calmly confront the person, try to talk things out, and clear up any misconceptions.

DATING

DATING

You know how I said earlier that my favorite part of school was the social aspect? Well, a major part of that is, of course, dating. This is the biggie that everyone wants to talk about 24/7. When I'm at school, I talk to my friends. When I'm at home, I talk to my mom. And let's face it, it's a topic most people love to discuss because it's fun to meet new people and explore new relationships.

I think I had my first boyfriend relationship when I was in kindergarten! I don't know why, exactly, but I've always had an interest in boys ever since I could remember. On my first day of kindergarten my mom walked me to school, and I was crying so hard because I didn't want to leave her. She kept saying, "Don't cry, honey. You're going to make lots of new friends."

Yep, it didn't take long. When my mom came to pick me up later that day, I was holding hands with this boy. I introduced him to my mom as my boyfriend, Scott. Poor guy. He lived down the street from me, and all he wanted to do was get away from me and go home! My mom was laughing, and she was, like, "Okay, Danielle. We'd better get home so you can tell me all about your first day of school." The second I let go of Scott's hand, he started running down the street. So I did what any normal four-year-old female would do in that situation — I chased him, caught him, slammed him up against the school fence, and kissed him. There you have it, my first official kiss and I didn't even know how to write my own name! My mom and I still laugh about that to this day.

I'm relieved to say I've mellowed a bit over the years and have curbed some of my more aggressive tendencies! In fact, I'm downright old-fashioned when it comes to relationships. I like it when the boy makes the first move and asks for the girl's number. And I like him to make the first call, not the other way around. I'll totally give a guy my number if he asks for it (provided I'm interested in dating him), but he has to make the first call. That doesn't mean I'm afraid to put the vibe out there. If I'm interested in someone, I'll let him know. It's very subtle, of course, like maybe striking up a conversation about a class or a teacher or a movie. Then we sort of take it from there.

As knowledgeable as I'd like to think I am when it comes to dating, I know I still have a lot to learn. I'm lucky I have great role models. My parents have a really solid relationship. They've been together since they were teenagers. High school sweethearts, in fact. So they've really taught me a lot just by being good examples. For one, they are really good at communicating with each other. I've learned that communication and honesty are the foundation of a successful relationship. If my mom has a problem with my dad or vice versa, they sit down and talk about things. And if something goes wrong, they don't point fingers and try to blame each other. I know this might sound a little corny, but they really respect each other. And I think that's what I've picked up from them. But I didn't learn it all overnight.

My first real crush, as in major, this-one-counts crush, was when I was a freshman in high school. I hadn't been in school most of the year because of *Boy Meets World*. But when the season ended in March, there I was, smack-dab in the middle of high school English every day. All of my friends had been talking about this guy Jeff, who was a senior. But I had no clue who he was because I hadn't been to school all year.

Anyway, I was sitting in English class and I noticed this incredibly beautiful guy sitting by the teacher's desk. My eyes locked on him, and I just had to know who he was. So I took it upon myself to make a little introduction. I strolled very confidently to the front of the room and just as I was about to say, "Hi, I'm Danielle. I don't think we've ever met," I noticed he was wearing a CTR ring. CTR is a Mormon symbol for "choose the right," and I knew this because my friend Jessica is a Mormon. Aha, I thought, now we have a little point of reference to talk about, something to break the ice. So I introduced myself to him, and he said his name was Jeff. I commented on his ring, and we totally hit it off! It didn't even register that this might be the Jeff all of my friends were raving about. Later that day, we saw each other in the hall and we talked some more. I pointed him out to one of my girlfriends, and she flipped out. She was, like, "Helloooooo, Danielle, that's the Jeff we were talking about!"

I usually don't care what other people think, but I was pretty psyched to know that Jeff had a solid reputation for being a good guy. And my gut told me he was a good guy, too. And he was. We started dating and, at first, it was a little awkward because he was eighteen and I was fourteen. I would come home from school and gush about him, and my mom would get this pained expression on her face. She was really worried that he was too old for me. But I convinced her that he was just right. And to prove it, I brought him home one day to meet the family and stay for dinner. I was right, everybody loved him.

Jeff and I were crazy about each other, inseparable at school and on the weekends. But we never kissed. I know that sounds strange, but for some reason I think we both had the age difference thing in the back of our heads. Maybe he didn't want to go too fast or make me feel uncomfortable by trying to kiss me and for sure I didn't want to make the first move because this was my first real relationship. So this kind of thing was all new to me. Looking back, I think Jeff knew I was a little too young to be romantically involved with an eighteen-year-old and he took things super-slow. And you know what? It was absolutely fine because I realized that when you're spending time with someone you really like, that kind of stuff doesn't matter at all. What matters is how well you get along, and Jeff and I got along great!

We'd hug and hold hands and go for ice cream and long walks. We'd pass notes in school, talk on the phone, go to the movies and dinner. We had such a great time together. One of the most romantic dates we ever had was when he called me up out of the blue one afternoon. He said, "Grab a jacket. I'll pick you up, and we'll go to the beach and watch the sunset." So we made a mad dash for the beach and we walked hand in hand along the shore. We took our shoes off, and he wrote my name in the sand with his feet. It was so fun and spontaneous! We were so wrapped up with what we were doing we totally missed the sunset — our whole reason for going! But that was a night I'll never forget.

There are so many romantic ways you can express your feelings for someone. When Jeff wrote my name in the sand, that meant more to me than any store-bought gift. I think it's the little things like that in a relationship that really go a long way, like writing someone a note or sending him a card, just because. If you're more inclined to verbalize your feelings, you can talk into a tape recorder and give a tape with a special message or call a person's answering machine and leave a message just to say you're thinking about him. My current boyfriend and I do these things for each other all the time, and we love it because it lets us know we're on each other's mind.

After Jeff graduated high school, he went away to college. We kept in touch, but, of course, our relationship ended. I wasn't sad, though, because I knew we'd stay friends (and we are).

It's funny — a lot of people think that because Ben Savage and I play boyfriend and girlfriend on the show we must be dating in real life. Well, here's the truth of the matter — we're really good friends and nothing more. Now, what's going to blow you away is that Ben was my first kiss — as far as real kisses go (my kindergarten smooch with Scott was nothing). Yes, can you believe I had to experience my first kiss on camera in front of a live studio audience, and then have it broadcast on national television for all the world to see?! I was twelve at the time, and it was basically my first scene with Ben. We both were so nervous because it was his first kiss, too. Ben almost threw up because he was so jittery. It was weird, to say the least, not to mention that we had to rehearse it all week. It was very methodical and not at all romantic the way I'd always imagined a first kiss would be. We've since kissed thousands of times, and you know what? It's no big deal. It's work. And no offense to Ben, who's one of my dearest friends. I'm sure if you asked him he'd say exactly the same thing.

So what's the difference between a kiss and a *kiss*? A lot. I've probably kissed Ben more than any other guy I've ever known. But it's work for us. Sure, we care about each other a lot, but we're friends. We're not interested in each other romantically. My first real kiss, other than that one with Ben, was with a real

DATING

boyfriend when I was older. That first real boyfriend kiss was very special because it was with someone I really liked. Remember the episode on *The Brady Bunch* when Bobby Brady gets his first kiss and he sees skyrockets? Well, I didn't see skyrockets, but I definitely had some fireworks going off! I felt all fluttery inside and I knew at that moment that what Ben and I were doing on the show was not real at all! When a kiss is the real deal, you know it. Trust me.

Some girls at my school think that kissing is no big deal. But I happen to disagree. I think it is a really special gift that two people exchange. I just don't kiss anyone, that's for sure. I made this promise to myself a couple of years ago that I would never kiss a boy just for the sake of kissing and this is why. What happened was, I had gone on a date with a guy, and it was perfectly fine. We went to the movies and grabbed a bite to eat afterward. Then we went back to my house and sat on the patio for a little bit and talked. I thanked him for the night and just before I went inside, I decided to kiss him. It was a really polite kiss, and I thought I was doing the right thing because, after all, he was a nice guy and we had a nice night. But as we were kissing, my mind started to wander off. *What should I wear tomorrow to the mall? My blue pants? That pink shirt?* It's horrible to say, but my mind just wasn't in the moment. And it completely sent the wrong message because there my date was, thinking that I was really into him. And there I was, counting down the seconds until I could shut the door and race up to bathroom to brush my teeth and go to bed.

I decided from that moment on that I would never allow myself to be in that situation again because it just wasn't real. I think that if you're not actually feeling the emotion to kiss somebody, you're going to regret it. My philosophy is never do anything you're going to regret.

I'm happy to say that I've had very few relationships that I regret. In fact, I'm really lucky that the guys I've dated have, for the most part, been pretty great. I think that comes from making the right choices about people. If you trust your instincts, you generally won't go wrong.

Random Thoughts

THINGS I'LL NEVER DO IN A RELATIONSHIP

1. Boss him around.

2. Act possessively or jealously.

3. Make him ditch his friends for me.

4. Act disrespectfully to his family.

5. Play mind games.

A HARD LESSON

A HARD LESSON

One time I didn't trust my gut and I ended up getting really hurt. A couple of years ago there was this guy who basically cheated on me. It's funny, a lot of people assume that because I'm an actress I can get any guy I want and that I never have any dating problems. I just snap my fingers and guys come running. That's so not true. I have problems dealing with life's little obstacles just like everyone else. This one was a major deal, let me tell you. If there's anything that will really damage a person's trust, it's cheating on him or her.

I was dating this guy for about two weeks. Now, I know that's not a terribly long time. But things were going really well, and I was just crazy about him. You know that excited "I can't wait to see this person" feeling you get when you're in a new relationship? Well, I had it big-time. I couldn't stop thinking about him and I couldn't wait to be with him.

When we first started dating, I full-on knew that he had a reputation for being a player. He had a different girlfriend practically every other week. But I went against that gut feeling and said to myself, *Danielle, this boy really likes you and has told you up front that he only has eyes for you. Enjoy this.*

He had totally convinced me that his reputation was a thing of the past and that he would be true to me. And why wouldn't I believe him? When somebody is looking at you square in the eyes and telling you how he feels, you should be able to trust what he's saying is true, right?

Winter break came around, and some of our friends were having holiday parties, and we went to a bunch of them together. On New Year's Eve, we went to a big party with all our friends, and it was there that he told me how happy he was with me and what a great girlfriend I was. In fact, he even told me he was starting to fall in love with me. I guess I was more than a little flattered by all of this praise. But on the inside, I was a little bit skeptical. I thought, *Huh? You're falling in love with me? We've only been dating a few weeks, and already you think you love me?*

My mom extended my curfew that night to one o'clock in the morning, so she came to pick me up at the party, and we went home. I couldn't help but feel I was going to miss out on something. But then again, it was one o'clock in the morning and I was exhausted. So off I went to bed, and you know what? I apparently *did* miss something. Something kind of big.

Apparently *he* decided to make friends with this girl who was visiting from out of town, and rumor had it that they hit it off, and he cheated on me after I left. Of course, I found this out from one of my friends and *not* from him. Big surprise. I felt so stupid and hurt. I was supposed to have dinner with him and his family a couple of nights after New Year's and it was all I could do to stay calm. After all, I thought it would be unfair of me not to give him the benefit of the doubt until we were able to talk one-on-one.

So the doorbell rang and there he was, ready to pick me up for dinner. I was kind of cold and aloof the whole ride over to his house. When we sat down for dinner with his family, I was not my usual talkative self and I think they noticed. Plus, I kept pushing the food around on my plate. I tried hard to put on a brave face, though I couldn't help but feel that what my friends said was true.

So after dinner I asked him point-blank, "Is it true you cheated on me on New Year's?"

He didn't even need to answer me because I could tell from his body language that it was true. His head dropped down a bit, and he took a deep breath. And then he admitted it. "It meant absolutely nothing," he told me. Meantime, all I could hear was my heart beating. He kept on apologizing, "I'll never do that again, Danielle, I swear."

"It's too late," I told him. "You've probably said this to every other girl you've ever cheated on. If you really cared about me, this kind of thing wouldn't have ever happened." Then I asked him to take me home. And he did, apologizing all the way in hopes that I would change my mind. But there was no way. I was stupid enough to fall for it the first time and I wouldn't let it happen again.

I was pretty crushed after that and I think it kind of zapped my confidence for a short while. When someone betrays you, you start to think, *Hmmm, am I that gullible? How did I let myself get into that kind of situation?* I blamed myself for getting cheated on. But in reality, it wasn't my fault at all. I don't know if he expected something from me and didn't get it so he looked elsewhere. I just know that now I'm very up-front with the guys I date. And for the most part, I tend to gravitate toward people who know how to treat another person. That's how I choose my friends and that's how I choose my boyfriends.

And when things aren't going well, whether it's in a friendship or a relationship, I've learned to speak up. I'm glad I did that with Mr. Cheater. If I hadn't stuck up for myself, I could have been in store for a lot more hurt and disappointment. A little guideline I try to follow is that I treat people the way I would want to be treated myself. Mr. Cheater is the exception to the rule, though. I didn't feel bad that things were ending between us. I felt bad that they had gone on so long.

When relationships end, it's never easy. But that's no reason to stay with someone. If the relationship is too one-sided, it's never going to work. You need to give and receive. Some people have the attitude that being with somebody is better than being with nobody. My opinion? Only a nobody would think that way.

I've dated guys who were really great for a while, but for whatever reason, we didn't continue because we discovered that we were at different places or had developed different interests and needs. And when that happens, you have to be honest, no matter what it is and no matter how much it hurts. You can't come up with fake excuses or reasons why you need to end things. And above all, you can't play games like not return his call for a week or avoid him at school. That's just wrong.

Sometimes I'm not the best talker in these situations. It's hard when something ends. But I really love to write. So at times, when I really need to express my feelings, I'll write them down in a letter, give the letter to that person, and have him read it while I'm there. Then we can talk about things. I've always respected and admired people who have been truthful with me and I know that the feeling was mutual.

There's no reason why things have to end on a sour note. Even after we've broken up, I've generally remained friends with the guys I've dated because we both were honest with each other. That doesn't mean the breaking-up part was easy. It just means that we had a respect for each other, so no matter what, we would be truthful with our feelings and considerate of the other person.

Random Thoughts

HOW TO GET INVOLVED IN YOUR COMMUNITY

It really doesn't take much to make a difference. Maybe you have a local Red Cross chapter where you can volunteer by giving blood or working in their office one day a week. Or you and your friends could get together and organize a food or clothing drive at your school. And what about all of those walk-a-thons and bike-a-thons? That's a great way to raise money for charity *and* get some exercise!

There are countless other ways to help, too. You could mow an elderly neighbor's lawn, read books to sick children in the hospital, get involved in an environmental project, deliver meals to the homeless. None of these things will take more than an hour out of your week, yet will undoubtedly have an impact on your community in a positive way. And you'd be surprised how much fun you can have, too. Give it a try!

ROLE MODELS

ROLE MODELS

Sometimes when I meet my fans, they tell me that I'm their role model. And that is *soooo* flattering. I always tell them I feel honored that they like the show and support me. It really means a lot. I don't mean to sound harsh or ungrateful for the compliments people bestow upon me. But I don't live my life to please others. I live my life to please me, my family, and God. When I go to sleep each night, I know that I am living a clean and healthy life that I am proud of. And it's nice to get that positive feedback from fans.

When I think of my own role models, though, I can't say any famous people come to mind. Sure, I admire other actors and actresses for their work. But I don't get excited by celebs, believe it or not. I don't know if it's because I work "in the business" or if it's just because I don't really watch a ton of TV or go to the movies a lot.

My role models have been *real* people — my parents and my late aunt Jackie. My mom and dad have sacrificed so much for

my brother and me. They parent by example. That is, they prac-
tice what they preach. And that means a lot to me because they
are so open-minded. Whenever I have a question, they take the
time to answer it. If they say no to something, I know that they
are willing to allow me to ask why. They've taught me right from
wrong. They've taught me it's better to give than to receive. And
they've always made me feel that my point of view counts. And
whenever they're wrong, they're not afraid to admit it. I hope
I'm half the parent to my kids that my folks are to me.

I see so many stories in the news where kids go bad. They
get into drugs and alcohol or steal or shoot one another. It's a
tragedy when this happens and it always makes me think how
hard it is for a parent to raise a child in today's world. I am so
fortunate to have the life that I have. And I'm not talking about
material things like new clothes or a fancy car. My life is complete because I have a family who loves me for me; a family who
cares about my well-being, no matter what; a family who has
encouraged me to dream and achieve things I once thought
were beyond my grasp.

The same can be said of my aunt Jackie, who passed away
last year. She was my mom's sister and probably one of my all-
time favorite people. You see, my aunt Jackie had kidney dis-
ease. She had been sick for fifteen years, practically my entire
life. Aunt Jackie had a way of making me feel like I was the
most important person in the world. Anytime I needed to talk,
she was there. When I was happy about something, she would
celebrate with me. And if I was upset about something, she

would comfort me and give me little pep talks about how special she thought I was. Not a day goes by that I don't think about her.

I remember one day when I was upset about something that happened at work. When I came home, I yapped about it endlessly to my mom and Aunt Jackie. They listened; they sympathized. And I just kept on yapping because to me it was such a big deal. What's funny is that when I look back on that day, I feel so silly. I mean, Aunt Jackie was sick, really sick. Her kidneys didn't function and she was on dialysis for a long time. She had to limit how much potassium she could have every day and how much liquid she could drink. Every day for her was such an ordeal, but she never once complained. Instead, she'd ask me how my day was. And I complained about the stupidest things. I can't even remember what it was that bugged me that particular day, it was so trivial.

Aunt Jackie taught me a lot about life by the way she lived. She embraced to the fullest every day she had. It's sad that death is what makes a person realize that life is the best gift we're given, despite the ups and downs we face along the way. I'm no expert, believe me. But I've learned to roll with the punches a little more and not let the little things in life get me down. I still have my moments, as we all do. And when that happens, I think of Aunt Jackie. Her courageous spirit lives on in me.

Random Thoughts
HOW IMPORTANT IS SCHOOL?

Please forgive me if I sound like a parent. But if you don't buckle down and make school a priority, chances are you're going to have a hard time succeeding in life. Hey, I'm not saying you have to get straight A's and discover the cure for cancer. But it's important to apply yourself fully to the work you're given each day. Life is full of challenges and only those who commit to trying their best will succeed. I truly believe this. Because I studied hard, I can do things like balance a checkbook, read the newspaper, and even speak a little Spanish. My parents always say that what you do with your mind is something that nobody can take away from you. I may not always be an actress and that's something that I'm comfortable with because that's only one of many things I know how to do. Simply put, there's no limit to what you can do if you open yourself up to learning.

RELIGION AND SPIRITUALITY

There used to be a time when the topic of religion didn't interest me. If somebody mentioned church or spirituality, I'd be, like, "Yeah, to each his own." I guess my indifference stemmed from when I was younger. My family and I used to go to a Catholic church together every Sunday. My parents were raised Catholic, so naturally my brother and I were, too.

Each church has its own customs and rituals, and my brother and I learned those of the Catholic religion, including making our First Holy Communion and our Confirmation. Those two very important rituals are ways in which Catholics affirm their faith. They are formal rites of passage, kind of like a bar or bat mitzvah for a Jewish person.

I remember vividly when I made my First Holy Communion the priest got upset with me. You see, when you're Catholic you have to do this thing called Confession. You go into this little room and have a conversation with the priest. You tell him all of your sins, like if you've been bad in school, or disrespectful to your parents, or if you've used swear words — stuff like that. It's the Church's way of cleansing you so that you can receive Communion. Communion is actually a little wafer about the size of a quarter that for Catholics represents the body of Christ, and it's part of every Mass.

After Confession, the priest tells you your penance — kind of like your punishment — which usually means you have to say a few prayers to complete the cleansing process. Well, anyway, every Catholic has to go to Confession before making his or her First Communion. So when I went in for the first time, the priest asked me, "Danielle, what are you going to confess?" And I said, "Well, Father (that's what you call the priest), I don't have anything to confess." And he said, "Sure you do. We all commit sins and therefore we all have something to confess." And I said, "I don't because I already confessed them to God."

Well, that didn't sit too well with him, and we had a long conversation about the Catholic religion. He understood that I had a personal relationship with God, and he even said that he did, too. But, he told me, "When you are in God's house (church, that is), you talk to Him and to me." I kind of understood what he was saying, like he was God's messenger in a way. So I ended up making my Holy Communion.

But deep inside, I guess I started to question whether this religion was right for me. How I knew that at eight years old I'll never understand. I just knew. Sunday after Sunday my family would go to church together, recite the Mass, and even though I was there, I felt like I was someplace else. My mind kept wandering, and I was just going through the motions. So I talked to my parents about it and I was surprised when I found out that they also had similar feelings about the Catholic religion.

When my family moved from Orange County to Los Angeles, we had to find a new church. My parents eventually stopped taking my brother and me to the Catholic church because they felt there were too many rules and the only reason they were raising us Catholic is because they had been raised Catholic. But when we stopped going to church, my parents felt guilty, so we started going to a Presbyterian church. But that didn't feel right to any of us, either. We tried a bunch of different churches, but none of them really stuck with me.

When my aunt Jackie passed away a couple of years ago, that was something that really jolted me into knowing there was something or someone beyond us. For God to have taken away somebody as wonderful as my aunt, there must have been a better place she was needed. Her death pushed me to want to know more, to want to explore.

My faith and spirituality have always been important to me. But for all my life, I thought there was some little thing that was missing. I can't say I have ever been able to put my finger on it. It's just that for as long as I can remember, I've questioned things. Even though I wasn't going to church for years, I was living a clean and healthy life that God would be proud of. I treated others as I would like to be treated. I loved and respected my family and obeyed my parents. I said my prayers every night before going to bed. I was a completely religious person without actually going to church.

About three months ago, I was talking with a couple of my friends who are older. They had told me about this Christian church that they really liked and said if I ever wanted to go to let them know. So one day, I took them up on their offer. And I've been going ever since. You know when you fit in some place and people share your beliefs. I felt right at home there, and it made me happier.

Now, the last thing I want to do is push my beliefs on somebody else. I have Jewish friends, Mormon friends, Protestant friends, and even nonreligious friends, and we all respect one another's beliefs. I've always thought that no matter what your religious affiliation, you should feel happy and fulfilled by it, not shamed and guilt-ridden.

I once knew a guy who was a born-again Christian, and he used to literally shove his religion down my throat. He would talk about it all the time and say that I *should* do this and I *should* do that. I'm a firm believer in freedom of expression, but he went overboard and it was a real turn-off. It was as if he was afraid of doing what *he* believed in. And he was trying to scare me into believing what he believed. Like I was a bad person if I didn't do this or that. You shouldn't feel like you have to abandon your personal beliefs for religion. It shouldn't feel like a chore. I think it's okay to question things and find what's right for you. That's how we grow and learn.

It's kind of interesting to me as an eighteen-year-old to realize how my needs and beliefs about religion and spirituality have changed from when I was eight. I go to church every Sunday now and I've never been happier. For that one hour each week, I take time to reflect upon my life, where I've been and where I'm headed. This church and its members accept me for who I am, and I walk away fulfilled and energized. Almost every Sunday when I go there, I end up bawling for the entire service because it feels so good to be there. It's such a release for me. They pass out prayer cards, and every week there is a group of people who get together, and all they do is pray for the people whose names are on the cards. I pray for my family and their safety, and for my friends and their families. And it's such a nice feeling to know that not only am I praying for this, but there's also a group of people that pray for the people I ask them to.

I took my brother to my church on Easter Sunday and he said he really liked it. I may end up taking the rest of my family there, too. But only if they want to go. My church is thirty minutes from my house. That's far to go, I know. But it's worth it to me because it's totally changed my life. Anything that makes you happy is something you must stick with.

Random Thoughts
PEER PRESSURE

If your friends are pressuring you to drink, or smoke, or stay out past your curfew, then you need to reevaluate your friends. Seriously, if they're really your friends, they won't pressure you, they'll respect you. And peer pressure isn't just about drinking and smoking. It's about cheating on a test, stealing a pack of gum from 7-11, and anything else you do because you think you have to belong to the "in" crowd. The times I've gone against what I believed in order to please someone else are times that I've deeply regretted. I would never coax someone into doing something they weren't comfortable with. And the people I call my friends would never do that to me. Remember those "Just Say No" advertisements? As simple as it sounds, there's no better way to respond to peer pressure than to remember those three words.

WHO I AM AND WHERE I'M GOING

WHO I AM AND WHERE I'M GOING

You've made it this far, so you pretty much know who I am and what I'm about. See, I told you at the beginning of this book that our worlds were pretty similar, didn't I? I'm not so different from you.

Like I said before, a lot of people see me on television and automatically think they know who I am and what I'm about. Just in case you didn't get it — Topanga Lawrence is not Danielle Fishel! Topanga is kind of a nit-picking nag, especially to Cory. Danielle is not like that at all. I'm much more carefree than Topanga, and much more fun!

But seriously, at the ripe old age of eighteen, I've been a lot of people. Maybe that doesn't make sense at first, but think about it. When I was twelve, I thought I knew it all. Then I turned thirteen, and I looked back at the girl I was at twelve and I realized I'd come a long way. I've thought I was all-knowing, all-important. And then I'd learn something totally out of left field that jolted me into reality. It's been that way ever since.

This last year and a half, I've completely come into my own as a young woman. I feel like I have a lot of things in life figured out and that's mostly because my family has guided me along but also allowed me the space to learn about myself. That's why I feel so proud and confident of who I am today.

I'm very aware of my strengths and weaknesses, where I want to go professionally and personally. My strengths are my ambition, my energy, my communication skills. I like people and I embrace them for their uniqueness. I love that not everyone is alike and I love learning about other people's backgrounds and beliefs. That's one of the world's greatest gifts.

And I suppose you want to know about my weaknesses. Well, I'm a, hmmm, I don't know how to say this, exactly. But, um, I'm a procrastinator! I'll put things off, especially chores or must-do tasks for as long as I can. One of my least favorite chores is cleaning up the pet poop, which meant Joey's cage in the house and the backyard because of Tyson. Uggh! I put that off for as long as I can.

Plus, I'm a pack rat. I save everything, even stupid little notes that I passed back and forth with my friends in the seventh grade. I have a junk drawer in my room with, like, five hundred notes in it that I've been meaning to clean out. (Because I procrastinate, I haven't done it yet.) And occasionally, I like to be lazy. Not lazy in the sense that I'm a lump on a log. But lazy like if I've been working really hard for a week and I finally have some time off, I just love to lie around in my pajamas. I turn off the ringer on the phone, close my bedroom door, and just hibernate.

I have my own car — well, actually, it's a sport utility vehicle — and sometimes I just love to get inside and drive and listen to music. I am a music freak! Depending on my mood, I'll plop in some rap or hip-hop or 'N Sync and just drive and sing at the top of my lungs. It's such a release for me to be in my own space and not worry about anyone else (well, of course I'm paying attention to the other cars). I can drive myself places and do things all by myself and you know what? I love it!

So what do these things have to do with knowing who I am and where I want to go? A lot, actually. My parents have always raised my brother and me to be leaders, not followers. In fact, one of my first sentences was "I'll do it by myself."

Something that I'm very proud of is my independence. It's so easy to do what the crowd is doing and not listen to your instincts. (Remember the chapter where I got grounded?) I used to spend so much time and energy trying to keep up with what everyone else was doing that I lost track of what I was about. I was such a social butterfly, on the phone with my friends, making plans even though I knew I was tired. I didn't want to miss a thing. But most of the time when we'd go out I'd realize that the only thing I was missing was sleep.

There came a time a couple of years ago in high school when I started to pull back. I had been dating this one guy for a short while and when we broke things off, I had the opportunity to date another guy. Well, I decided that I wanted to have some time alone. And I was tired of socializing just for the sake of socializing. So I stayed home one Friday night and read a book. I loved it! Then I did it the following weekend. Then I ventured out on my own to the movies. I treated myself to a frozen yogurt and a walk on the beach. Alone! It was great.

I started reflecting on myself, my future, what kind of person I was, and what kind of person I wanted to become. I watched families play in the sand, kids laughing. I saw a guy wearing a UCLA sweatshirt, doing his homework at a picnic table. It made me think that my life can take so many different directions. So why limit myself? I mean, what I was doing with my friends was basically limiting myself. I love them dearly, but my life was becoming very one-dimensional.

The same goes for acting. I love it, but I'm also realistic enough to know that I may not be doing this forever. One day you're on top and the next day you're not. That's just the business. So I've started to explore my other interests. I know I want to go to college someday and study psychology and get into long debates with my fellow students about world peace.

I want to get married and have kids someday and make peanut-butter-and-jelly sandwiches for their lunches and build sand castles on the beach. And what I've always wanted to do, believe it or not, is be a waitress! I love serving other people and I think that would be the coolest job! I swear I will do that some- day, you'll see!

Just so you know, I still enjoy a good night out on the town with my friends. I do. And maybe I'll have an incredible acting career that will span three more decades. You never know. But one thing I'm certain I can bank on now is that these things are not the be-all and end-all. It's good to listen to all types of music once in a while, know what I mean? And if you find that you march to the beat of several different drums, so much the better.

ABOUT THE AUTHOR

Monica Rizzo is a Los Angeles-based staff correspondent for *People* magazine. Her work has also appeared in *Teen People, Seventeen, YM, McCall's* and *Nickelodeon*.